SCIENCE FUN WITH DRUMS, BELLS, AND WHISTLES

Rose Wyler
Pictures by Pat Stewart

JULIAN MESSNER ■ NEW YORK
A Division of Simon & Schuster, Inc.

Text copyright © 1987 by Rose Wyler
Illustrations copyright © 1987 by Pat Stewart
All rights reserved including the right of reproduction in whole or in part in any
form. Published by Julian Messner, a Division of Simon & Schuster, Inc.,
Simon & Schuster Building, Rockefeller Center, 1230 Avenue of the Americas,
New York, NY, 10020

JULIAN MESSNER and colophon are trademarks of Simon & Schuster, Inc.

Designed by Lisa Hollander
Manufactured in the United States of America

10 9 8 7 6 5 4 3 2 1 Lib. ed.
10 9 8 7 6 5 4 3 2 1 Pbk. ed.

Library of Congress Cataloging-in-Publication Data
Wyler, Rose.
Science fun with drums, bells, and whistles.

Summary: Instructions for a variety of simple experiments involving sound.
1. Sound—Experiments—Juvenile literature.
2. Scientific recreations—Juvenile literature.
(1. Sound—Experiments. 2. Experiments. 3. Scientific recreations) I. Stewart, Pat
Ronson, ill. II. Title.
QC226.6.W95 1987   534   87-7838
ISBN 0-671-63783-5 Lib. ed.
ISBN 0-671-64760-1 Pbk. ed.

FOREWORD

Science is a special kind of knowledge. It explains how the world around us works.

Ever since early times people have been asking "Why is the sky blue?" or "What makes a seed begin to grow?" or "What makes sound and music?" People have always thought and talked about these questions. But you can do real science experiments to help you find answers.

This book will show you how to do experiments yourself with your own homemade musical instruments. The activities are easy to do and are lots of fun. They lead to many exciting discoveries. Try them.

Lewis Love
Great Neck Public Schools
Long Island, New York

ACKNOWLEDGMENTS

The author and publisher wish to thank the people who read the manuscript of this book and made suggestions: Gerald Ames; Lewis Love, Great Neck Public Schools; Claudia and Sam Zaslovsky; and the many young "helpers" who tried the experiments.

Science Fun Books

Science Fun with Drums, Bells, and Whistles
Science Fun with a Homemade Chemistry Set
Science Fun with Mud and Dirt
Science Fun with Peanuts and Popcorn
Science Fun with Toy Boats and Planes

CONTENTS

Drums—Rat-a-Tat-Tat, Boom!   7
Make a Drum ● How a Sound Starts ● Tom-toms ● Tone Tests ●
Bongo Beat ● Drumming a Story ● The Drums in Your Ears

Ring Out the Bells   17
Coffee-can Bell ● Bell Shapes ● Gong Experiments ● Jingle
Bells ● Nail Chimes ● Musical Glasses

Whistles and Horns   29
How Whistles Work ● Soda-straw Whistles ● Flutes: Old and
New ● Why a Horn Honks ● Tuning Homemade Horns ● Horns
in Bands

Noise and Music   41
What Makes a Noise a Noise? ● Picturing Sound Waves ●
Orchestra Sounds ● Combo Concert

Drums—Rat-a-Tat-Tat, Boom!

Wide drums, narrow drums, short drums, tall drums—there are so many kinds of drums.

The big bass drum booms; the small drums go rat-a-tat-tat. They make you feel like marching. Listen to bongo drums and you want to dance.

Why do different drums sound different? And why does a drumbeat sound different from the toot of a horn or the clang of a bell?

You can find out. Make some drums and play them. Make bells, whistles, and horns, too. This book tells you how. It is a book of science experiments you can hear.

Make a Drum

Anybody can play a drum. Anybody can make one, too. Long ago, cave dwellers used drums. At first they just beat on a hollow log. Then they fixed an animal skin over the log to make a drumhead.

Today, a drum still has two parts: a shell and a drumhead. The shell can be anything hollow, even a bowl or jar. The drumhead can be a sheet of anything that stretches.

Try using an empty can for a drum shell. A coffee can works well. For the drumhead take a round balloon. Cut off the neck. Stretch the rest over the can opening and make it fit tight. Put a rubber band around it to hold it in place. And there's your drum!

To play the drum, sit and hold it between your knees. For a drumstick, use a pen or pencil, or try your fingers.

A bone makes a good drumstick too. Clean and dry the big leg bone of a chicken. Beat your drum with it and you'll know why a chicken leg is called a drumstick.

Animal bones were used as drumsticks by cave people. Maybe they beat their big drums with bones from wild horses. Imagine how that sounded—boom, BOOM, BOOMM!

How a Sound Starts

You can hear the sound of a drum, but you can't see the sound. What goes on? What happens when a sound starts?

Beat your drum and gently touch the drumhead. Your finger tips tingle because the drumhead is shaking—it is *vibrating*. Touch the side of the drum and you find that it is vibrating too. Sprinkle some dry cereal on the drumhead. Beat it and vibrations make the cereal jiggle.

The vibrations spread through the air around the drum. They make waves in the air that are like waves in water. You can't see these waves. But when they reach your ears, you hear sound.

You know how to make a drum sound louder, don't you? Strike it hard and you get strong vibrations. Tap it lightly and the vibrations are weak. The drum sound is faint.

When a sound is faint, it's because the sound waves are small. When sound waves are big, the sound is loud. The more energy that is used in making the waves, the bigger they are.

Tom-toms

American Indians made wonderful drums. In many tribes, the favorite drum was the small wooden tom-tom. People danced to its beat at meetings and feasts.

You can make your own tom-tom, using a wooden bowl for the shell. Stretch plastic over the top and tape it in place. When you play the tom-tom, hold it in one hand and the drumstick in the other. Do you like the sound?

The tom-tom sounds different from a tin-can drum. That's because it has a wooden shell. Wood vibrates in its own special way, giving a sound that comes only from wood.

Tone Tests

It's easy to change the way a drum sounds. Tighten the drumhead and the tone goes higher.

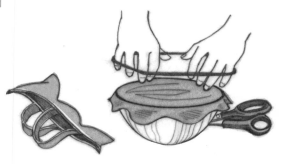

Try this. Make a drum using a bowl for the shell and plastic from a bag for the drumhead. Stretch the bag across the top of the bowl and hold it in place with a rubber band. Set your drum on a table and test its sound. Then pull down the plastic. Make it fit tighter and you'll get a higher tone. For a lower tone, loosen the plastic.

A tight drumhead springs back faster than a loose one. It vibrates at a faster rate and that makes the tone higher.

The drum in a band must always be in tune. Screws around the rim are used to tighten the drumhead. When it's time to strike up the band, the drum is ready.

The big drums lead the parade. Then come the smaller drums. Why are drums of different sizes used? Test big and little drums and you'll hear the answer.

Make drums from cans of different sizes. Use balloons for drumheads and make them fit tight. Play each drum with the same drumstick.

You'll hear lower tones from the big drums. They vibrate at a slower rate because of their size.

Bongo Beat

Tie a big drum and a little drum together and play them with your hands. That's how bongo drums are played. Each of the two drums has a different tone. You might hear bongo drums played on a Caribbean island.

Drumming a Story

Long ago, in Africa, the drum had an important use. A big drum was kept in the center of a village, under a shed. It was called the "talking drum." People sent messages on it by playing signals that stood for words.

Your drums aren't talking drums, but they can help you tell a story. Try *The Three Bears*. Beat a big drum along with Father Bear's words. Use a smaller drum for Mother Bear's words, and a very small drum for Baby Bear.

Make up other drum stories. You can say a lot with drums, since big drums have lower tones than small ones.

The Drums in Your Ears

Do you know you have two drums inside your body? These drums are in your ears. Each is a little sheet of skin that is tightly stretched. When sound waves reach it, the skin acts just like a drumhead. It vibrates, and you hear the sound.

Here's a way to see what happens. Take one of your tin-can drums and have a grown-up cut off the bottom. Put bits of dry cereal on the drumhead. Then ask a friend to hold the can above his face and say "Rat-a-tat-tat." Watch the bits of cereal jiggle as the drumhead vibrates. The sound makes your eardrums vibrate too, and you hear "Rat-a-tat-tat."

Ring Out the Bells

Listen to them—bike bells, door bells, school bells, sleigh bells. They jingle, buzz, and clang.

You would never mistake the ring of a bell for the boom of a drum. Yet both sounds start when one thing hits another. A drumstick hits the drum; a clapper hits the bell.

But the bell doesn't boom, it *rings*. Why is this? Why does a bell *ring*?

Coffee-can Bell

Do you still have your coffee-can drum? You can change it into another kind of noisemaker—a clanging bell.

Take off the drumhead. Then ask a grown-up to punch a hole in the bottom of the can. For the clapper, use a metal nut or button. Tie it to a string and thread the string through the hole. Let the clapper dangle so it can hit the inside of the can. Now tie a knot in the string or add a dab of clay to hold it in place.

Shake the can and it clangs. It rings like a cowbell. And that's what it is—a real bell.

Why is a bell sound so different from a drum sound? A drumhead is soft. When it is hit, it shakes up and down and the drum booms. But your bell is made of metal. When it is struck, the metal doesn't give very much. It stays stiff. As it vibrates, it makes a special sound—it rings.

Your bell clangs. Will the sound change if you shorten the clapper string? Try a different clapper too. Try changing the shape of the can by pressing the sides together a little. Does the bell still clang?

No matter what you do to your bell, it will sound tinny. That's because it is made of tin-can metal. If you want a different sound, find a bell made of some other metal.

Bell Shapes

Your coffee-can bell might sound better if it had a narrow top and flaring sides. Many bells are shaped that way. Inside the clapper strikes near the rim. Strike that kind of bell on the top, the side, and the rim. You will find that the clearest sound comes from near the rim.

A clay flower pot is shaped like a bell. It will ring like one too if you put a clapper inside.

For a clapper, tie a metal nut to a string. Then run the string through the hole of an empty flower pot. Let the nut hang so it will strike near the rim. Fix the string in place with modeling clay. Now shake the bell. It rings because pottery vibrates the way metal does.

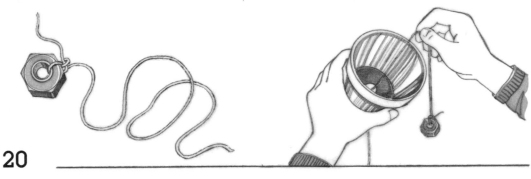

Not all bells are cup-shaped. School bells and bike bells are shaped like saucers. But they too have clappers that strike near the rim.

Gong Experiments

A gong has no clapper. You hit it near the rim with a rod and it rings with a beautiful tone.

Tie a long thread on the handle of a metal spoon, and you have a gong. Dangle the spoon, strike it with another spoon, and the gong rings. Its sound is rich. You can make the gong sound even better and louder. Strike it while you hold the thread against your ear. Now you hear a loud GONGGG! Why does it sound so loud?

The ringing of the gong causes stronger vibrations in the thread than in the air. The vibrations are so strong you can feel them. They make your fingers tingle. The weight of the spoon draws the thread tight and sound waves go through it easily.

Tie a cloth strip to the spoon and repeat the experiment. Now the gong doesn't sound loud. Although cloth is made of thread, it can't be pulled tight. So it's a poor path for sound.

Test other materials—yarn, wire, plastic, paper. You'll find sound goes through some of them better than others. As a rule, firm materials make the best paths for sound.

Jingle Bells

What makes jingle bells jingle? Take one apart and you will find a little ball inside. When you shake a jingle bell, the ball rattles around, striking against the metal. The bell is really a rattle that rings.

Everyone likes to hear jingle bells. In summer they announce ice cream trucks. In winter they are sleigh bells, and you can put them on your ice skates.

If you tie jingle bells on your cat's collar, you can keep track of the pet. Birds can too—and they'll keep away from the cat.

Nail Chimes

Now listen to some nails. Tie some nails of different sizes on a string. Shake the string and the nails jingle like chimes. You hear a mixture of tones.

Why are there so many different tones? Do big nails sound different than small ones?

Line up the nails according to size. Ask a grown-up to help you drive the nails part way into a strip of wood. Then tap each one with a large nail to make it ring. Which nail has the lowest tone? The biggest one?

A big nail has more metal in it than a small one. So it vibrates at a slower rate. That makes its tone lower. How high or low a tone sounds is called *pitch.*

Hold the wooden strip by one end and tap the nails. Now you're playing a little bell lyre—ding, dong, ding!

The bell lyre in a band has a frame with different size metal strips set across it. Each strip vibrates at a different rate, sounding a different tone in the scale. The tones are bell-like, but they have the same pitch as those notes from a piano.

Musical Glasses

You can get music from glasses too. Tap a glass along the side and at the rim. The clearest sound comes from near the rim. The glass rings like a bell, doesn't it?

Not all glasses have the same tone. Use a pen to tap glasses of different sizes and listen to the difference in their tones. You'll find that the large and thick glasses have a low tone. Only thin glasses have a high-pitched tinkle.

When water is in a glass, the glass sounds as if it were thicker. It vibrates at a slower rate and rings with a lower tone, as this experiment shows.

Tap an empty glass with a pen to make it ring. Then pour some water in it and tap it again. The tone is lower now, isn't it? Pour in more water and it becomes lower still. The more water you add, the lower the tone.

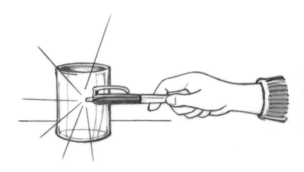

26

You can get a range of tones from glasses the same size. Just pour different amounts of water in them. Then tap the glasses and you can play a tune.

Line up five glasses of the same size. Put different amounts of water in them, as shown in the picture. Starting with the first glass, tap each one. Do you hear a scale—do, re, mi, fa, sol? Try to play *Mary Had a Little Lamb*. You know how it goes:

Mary had a little lamb, little lamb, little lamb.
Mary had a little lamb; its fleece was white as snow.

To play the tune, tap the glasses in this order:

3 2 1 2 3 3 3,
2 2 2, 3 5 5
3 2 1 2 3 3 3;
3 2 2 3 2 1

Try other tunes too and hear the glasses sing!

To check the pitch of the glasses, try matching their tones with notes played on a piano. Piano keys are attached to strings of different lengths. Hit a key and its string vibrates at a certain rate. When a glass vibrates at that rate, its pitch is the same as the note from the piano.

Start with the glass that plays *do*. While you tap it, have a friend play middle C on the piano. Do the tones match? If the pitch is too low, take some water out of the glass with a spoon. If it's too high, add water. Now match the *re* glass to D on the piano. Then check the next glasses with the next notes.

Mark the water levels on the glasses, so you can refill them quickly. Then you'll be able to make the glasses sing again and again.

28

Whistles and Horns

When you blow a whistle or a horn, what happens? Air inside it vibrates and sound starts. This may seem simple, but is it? Just how do you get the kind of sound you want?

Does a long whistle sound different from a short one? Why do big horns sound different from small ones? How can you make a horn play different tones?

You can find out from experiments with homemade whistles and horns. Will anyone mind the noise? No, not if you tell them that you are blowing and tooting for science.

How Whistles Work

Listen to a toy whistle, the kind with a long tube. Then listen to a short whistle, the kind a gym teacher uses. The short whistle sounds much higher. Why is that?

A short whistle has a small air space. When you blow into it, the air inside vibrates very fast. That causes a high tone. Blow a long whistle and you blow one with more air inside. The air doesn't vibrate as fast and the tone is lower.

It doesn't matter what vibrates—air, metal, or glass. A small amount vibrates faster than a large amount and gives a higher tone.

Soda-straw Whistles

Of course you have sucked soda through a straw. But did you ever blow into a straw and make it whistle?

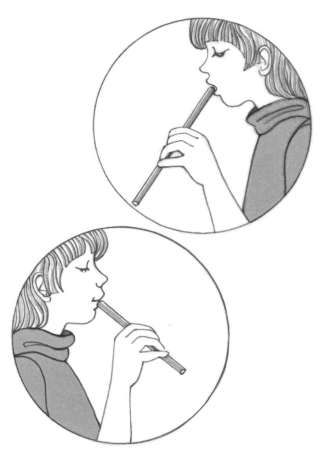

Try this. Take a straight plastic soda straw. Hold one end against your lower lip. Tilt the other end a little. Now blow into it gently. Toot-toot—the straw is a whistle!

Can you change the sound? Cut off a piece and blow through the straw again. Its pitch is higher now, isn't it? You will get an even higher tone if you blow through the short piece. How high a tone can you get?

A soda-straw whistle works like other whistles. The shorter it is, the higher its pitch.

Try this too. Blow through a straw, then put your finger on the bottom and blow again. Now the tone is lower. Jiggle your finger and the sound goes up and down. Your whistle warbles.

If you have a pet bird, warble for it with your whistle. Maybe the bird will join you and warble too.

Why does a whistle sound different when it's closed than when it's open? Closing the tube slows down the vibrations of the air in it. That lowers the pitch.

You can also warble with a short straw and a long straw. Hold them both up to your mouth and blow through one, then the other. To warble three tones, use three straws of different lengths. Try four straws too.

To handle four straws, line them up according to length. Put a ring of modeling clay on each one and stick them together. Now blow all the whistles, moving them back and forth, and four notes blend. Do you like the sound?

Your set of whistles is like a panpipe, an ancient instrument. In South America, today, the panpipe is played by Indians in many villages. It is made of bamboo and used to play lovely old songs and lively new ones.

Flutes: Old and New

Some years ago scientists dug up a strange bone that cave people had used. The bone was hollow and had six holes along the side. What could it be? The scientists found out when one of them blew through it. Using his fingers to close one hole after another, he got six different tones. The cave people had learned how to get different tones from a single tube. They had invented the flute!

Some of the flutes used today are like those of the cave people. The tube is made of bamboo or plastic. The player blows across one end, closing and opening the holes with his fingers. Perhaps there's one of these simple flutes in your school. If you can get one, try to tootle the scale on it.

The holes on a flute are called stops. Opening any one of them is like cutting off the tube at that point. Blow a flute with the first stop open and only the air above it vibrates. You get a high tone.

Close the stop and open the second one. Blow the flute again. Now more air vibrates and the tone is lower. Run your fingers down the tube closing the holes one after another and you run down the scale.

The flute used in orchestras is blown through a hole in the side, and the stops are opened and closed by metal keys. Beautiful music is played in this way. Yet the flute is just a long whistle with holes.

Why a Horn Honks

A horn is somewhat like a whistle. It's a tube that makes a sound when you blow into it. But its shape is different. The horn gets wider and flares at one end to make it sound louder. The mouthpiece is different too.

Look inside the mouthpiece of a toy horn and you see a thin flap. The flap is called a reed. When you blow the horn, the reed vibrates. This makes the air in the tube vibrate, and the horn honks.

Use a dab of modeling clay to stick the flap in a horn to the mouthpiece. The clay will keep the flap from vibrating. Now try to blow the horn. All you hear is your breath.

Tuning Homemade Horns

You can make a horn from a soda straw that's almost as loud as a party horn. The straw can be paper or plastic, straight or the kind that bends.

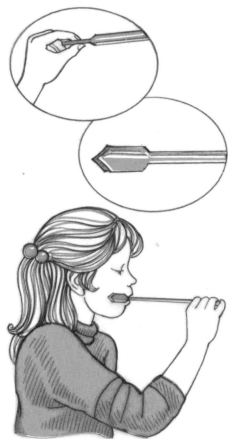

Pinch one end of a straw to flatten it. Flatten about three-quarters of an inch. Snip off each corner so there are two flaps at the end. Open them a little and they'll work like reeds. Now your straw is a horn. Put the reed end in your mouth, but let your lips touch only the round part of the straw. Blow hard and the horn honks.

What happens if you shorten the tube? Will the pitch go up? Cut off one piece, then another, and listen for the answer.

To check the pitch of a straw horn, ask a friend to play a note toward the middle of a piano while you blow. If the horn pitch is lower and doesn't match the piano note, snip off a bit of the straw. If it's still too low, snip off another bit. Keep on doing this until the horn and piano sound the same tone.

Eight straw horns can be cut and tuned to play a scale of eight notes. If you can get a group together to make and blow the horns, try some songs. Ask each player to take care of two horns, holding one in each hand. Start with something slow and easy, like *Twinkle, Twinkle, Little Star.* Try *On Top of Old Smokey* too. What other songs will you play?

Horns in Bands

Here's another way to change the pitch of a straw horn. Cut a hole in the side and the horn will sound as if it were cut off at that point.

Pick a place for the hole and pinch the straw there. Then cut a notch in the flattened part. After the straw springs back into shape, blow through it. Hear how high it sounds.

To lower the pitch, cover the hole with a finger and blow the horn. Cut a second hole in it and test it. Try more holes, too. How many tones can you get from the horn?

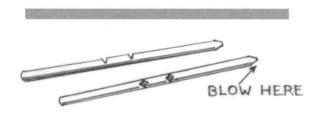

BLOW HERE

The horns in jazz bands have holes that are opened and closed by keys. Yet horn playing is difficult. Fast fingering is needed for fast tunes.

Most of the horns used in marching bands also have holes with keys. Some horns have very long tubes. The longer the tube, the deeper the tone of the horn.

Take a straw horn and tape a second one on the end. Hear how low it sounds. Then tape on a third straw. If you use three straws that bend, the horn will be easy to handle. And it will be somewhat like a horn with a long coiled tube.

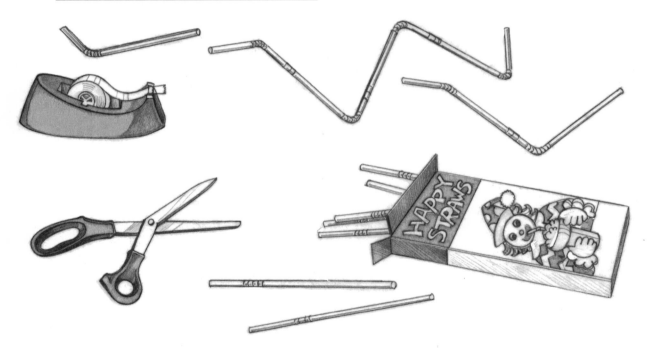

By now you and your friends must have lots of horns. Try blowing them all together. You'll have a blast!

Noise and Music

What a lot of different sounds you can make with your drums, bells, whistles, and horns! You can get high and low tones from them and you can play them loud or soft.

When you like the sound you have made, you call it music. When you don't like it, you call it noise. People say that about sounds from real instruments too. But what is the difference between noise and music?

What Makes a Noise a Noise?

In music, the tones are related in some way. The vibrations making a certain note may be twice as fast as those in the next note. Or they may be half as fast. Or they may be repeated from time to time. The tones go up and down and form a pattern that you can follow.

In drum playing, the tones may not change but the rhythm does. As slow and fast drum beats form a pattern, you hear drum music, not just noise.

In noise, tones are not related. When you have a blast of horns, tones are jumbled together, helter-skelter. There isn't any pattern.

Picturing Sound Waves

Although no one can see sound, it's possible to get pictures of sound waves. Only outlines show on the pictures, but they help explain differences in sound.

To make the pictures, scientists use a special machine that looks like a television set. Sound from an instrument is sent into a microphone and broadcast. Then vibrations from the sound are picked up by the set and appear on the screen as lines.

When the sound is high-pitched, the lines form narrow waves that are close together. A low-pitched sound forms wide waves that are far apart. Loud and faint sounds with the same pitch make waves that have the same shape. But if the tones are loud, the waves are big. If tones are faint, the waves are small.

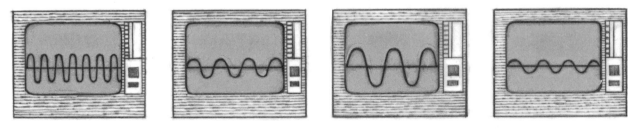

HIGH   LOW   LOUD   SOFT

The wave shape for any one note is always the same. By timing the waves, scientists can tell the number of vibrations per second that make each note. Any note you blow makes the horn vibrate over a hundred times a second. Amazing, isn't it?

Orchestra Sounds

The next time you see and hear an orchestra, notice the instruments. You can't help thinking of the things you have learned about them.

You know that a big area vibrates slowly. That's why drums and other big instruments have low tones. Air in long tubes vibrates slowly too. And so the horns with long tubes are low-pitched. Short horns are high-pitched.

At times different instruments play the same note. Horns, flutes, and violins—perhaps thirty or more of them—are vibrating at exactly the same rate. At other times the different instruments play different notes. The tones blend and the sound is wonderful—it's music.

Combo Concert

Your homemade instruments look altogether different from those in an orchestra. Yet music can be played on them. Tunes can be played on a set of glasses and on soda-straw horns of different sizes. Homemade drums can be used for exciting rhythms.

Play all the instruments together with your friends and start a combo. You'll like the sound if you try some tunes. After practicing them you'll want to give a concert.

On the program you can include a drum story, and perhaps dances with bongos and tom-toms. For a number with bells, try *Jingle Bells.*

A good opening number is *Mary Had a Little Lamb.* After the horn players play the tune, tap it on the musical glasses and then have the entire combo play it together. If you sing along with the glasses, change the words to:

Have some science fun with us, noisy fun, noisy fun;
Have some science fun with us, testing different sounds.

Of course, you and your friends will have ideas too. If you keep the music simple, the concert will be great. Be ready to bow when you hear the applause!

Save your homemade drums, bells, and horns for you will probably be asked to repeat the program.

Your sound-makers are not real musical instruments, but they are real science equipment. You can keep on having *Science Fun* with them, doing experiments you can hear.